TOPKAPI
PALACE

REHBER
BASIM YAYIN DAĞITIM
REKLAMCILIK VE TİCARET A.Ş.

Introduction

Welcome to Turkey, and welcome to the city of Istanbul.

Istanbul is the most beautiful city in Turkey and one of the most beautiful cities in the whole world. It is the one and only city to be located on the junction of two continents, Europe and Asia. It is the one and only city to have been the capital of two great world empires over a period of nearly 2,000 years. It is a treasure trove of history that enriches, not only Turkey, but the whole of the Old World!

Now one of the greatest of the world centers of culture, art, history, commerce and trade, Istanbul first made its appearance on the world stage at the end of the 2nd millennium B.C. as a small fishing village by the name of Lygos. In the 7th century B.C. it was settled by a group of Megarians led by the commander Byzas, after whom the new settlement, Byzantium, was named. The city developed very rapidly, thanks

to an excellent geographical location which allowed it to control all military and commercial activities between the Black Sea and the Mediterranean, and to the presence of an excellent natural harbour in the Golden Horn. In the following centuries, the city attracted the attention of all the peoples and nations throughout Anatolia, coming under the hegemony of various different states, until finally, in the first half of the 4th century, the Emperor Constantine the Great proclaimed the city the eastern capital of the Roman Empire and changed its name to Constantinopolis. With the establishment of Christianity as the state religion, Constantinopolis emerged as the capital of the Byzantine Empire. The finest creations of the great empire founded by the Byzantines were produced in this city, which was soon adorned with scores of the most beautiful and the most magnificent buildings of the time. Although, in the 11th century, the Byzantine Empire found itself unable to keep up with the Renaissance movement in Western Europe and entered a period of rapid decline, it still succeeded in preserving

the creations of the earlier periods. After the conquest of the city by
the Turks in 1453, the young Sultan Mehmet II very wisely issued
orders for the careful preservation of all surviving Byzantine buildings.
The fact that he was a great connoisseur of art undoubtedly played a
decisive role in his decisions, and in spite of the Islamic prohibition on
all forms of representation of the human figure he had his own portrait
painted by the distinguished Italian painter Bellini, thus initiating a
long and fruitful artistic tradition. In ordering the preservation of the
Byzantine works of art he was acting as a very wise and pragmatic

Palace at night.

statesman. Having made this city the capital of their empire, the Ottomans were to rule for several decades over an extraordinarily colorful and multi-ethnic mosaic in which the Greeks formed the majority of the population. The fundamental aim of the Ottoman rulers was to exert their hegemony without arousing apprehension or unease in the other ethnic groups. The secret at the heart of their success in creating a great empire that was to rule for over 600 years over a vast territory extending from the Atlantic to the Indian Ocean lay in their being able to live in an atmosphere of peaceful co-existence with with nearly 100

different ethnic groups. The Ottomans never interfered with the language or beliefs of the peoples over whom they ruled, and never at any time attempted a policy of assimilation. As a result, great churches and monuments of secular and military architecture were preserved and maintained, and were thus able to survive over the centuries.

In the period of over 1,000 years during which it functioned as the capital of the Byzantine Empire, this extraordinarily beautiful city had been adorned, as we have mentioned above, with masterpieces created

by a great civilization. It was only natural, however, that the Turks should wish to give it a more obviously Turkish atmosphere and endow it with an essentially Muslim character. Thus it was that, while still conserving the old Byzantine buildings, they filled all four corners of the city with the finest products of their own artistic and architectural genius. This was to result in the creation of a city in which the masterpieces of Byzantine art and architecture were combined with the beauties created by the Ottomans, transforming the city into one of the

Topkapı Palace and Golden Horn.

9

richest open-air museums in the world. That is why we have decided, in preparing this little book on Topkapı Palace, one of the most important, indeed perhaps the most important of all the museums in the city, to include some of the mosques of extraordinary beauty to which the city owes its peculiarly Turkish and Islamic atmosphere. Before we concentrate on the Topkapı Palace, it will be appropriate to

Above: Justice or Sultan's pavilion.

Below: Courtyard and pool.

take a look at the palace architecture and the general rules of architecture in the Ottoman Empire. The Ottoman sultans and chieftains lived under very modest circumstances starting with 1299 when Osman Bey, the founder of the Ottoman dynasty, refused to pay tax to Konya, the capital of the Anatolian Seljuk State, and founded an independent state. The sources on the founding years of the Ottoman state do not refer to any " palace" tradition at all. We can assume that they lived in big mansions for almost a century and a half until the conquest of İstanbul in 1453. But those residences were neither palaces nor castles in the western sense. The sultans and chieftains of those times, who were also the heads of state, had not lost the common touch either;

they used to pray together with their subjects. Building a " sultan's lodge" in the mosques where the sultan had to pray alone out of security reasons became a rule only after the conquest and the rapid growth of a mighty empire.

Radical changes in the organization of the state and the birth of a " palace" tradition, which the originally nomadic Turks of Central Asia did not have, coincided with the emergence of the "converts" as the ruling class. These subjects who were mostly schooled as Janissaries and were the loyal servants of the sultan replaced the viziers and grand viziers coming from the Turkish nobility and took over the state affairs. Although we do not have adequate evidence, it is reasonable to assume that the sultans and chieftains who ruled prior to the conquest of İstanbul also led a rather pompous life in their mansions and kept a number of servants for their security and service. But after the conquest, the number of servants in various palaces grew to such an extent, that it was not extraordinary to have 400 people serving in a palace kitchen as we will also see later on! The number of civil servants and guards who attended the council meetings even reached ten thousand! The "Enderun" which was both school and the initial office of the prospective civil servants was an integral part of the sultan's palace and thus caused the number of palace inhabitants to reach large numbers. The " Harem", on the other hand, used to be a phenomenon by itself too. The circumcision ceremonies of the princes were held in the harem, and there were times when the number of guests exceeded 15 thousand. The Council of the pre-conquest era which used to be the place where the sultans and chieftains came together with the common people and gave an ear to their needs and wishes, became a secluded institution of the Palace as the sultan became " the shadow of God on earth", a person in a golden cage who had no contact to his subjects. Consequently, the not so large residence of the rulers during

the founding years of the empire was replaced by an oversized palace that extended on a huge area. Topkapı Palace served as the residence of the Ottoman dynasty for some three and a half centuries. Occupying a large site at the end of the historical peninsula, it has nothing in common with the traditional Western concept of a royal palace. There is no attempt whatever at architectural unity. Each succeeding sultan would make his own additions and modifications, so that individual sections were continually being demolished or transformed. As most of the buildings were of wood, the palace was as greatly affected as the city itself by the great conflagrations that broke out at frequent intervals, causing severe damage to several sections of the palace and the loss of their own peculiar original style. When these sections were rebuilt, the harmony with the surviving sections which they had probably once displayed was now lost. Moreover, after the transfer of the royal residence to Dolmabahçe the whole congeries of buildings of which Topkapı Palace was composed fell into general neglect and dilapidation while, at the same time, during the construction of the railroad along the coast, a number of the old pavilions were demolished and others cut off from the gardens to which they had formerly been

On the left :
The Blue Mosque.

On the right :
Saint Sophia.

joined. Thus it is that any visitor to Topkapı Palace today who seeks to find a certain artistic or architectural unity will be severely disappointed. Topkapı Palace owes its importance to the extraordinary beauty and wealth of the collections which it contains. Yes, the Topkapı Palace has no architectural style but Ottoman architecture has succeeded in becoming a very original school which perfectionized the Seljuk architecture preceding it, and which produced unsurpassed works of art especially in the 16th century. The civilian Ottoman architecture flourished constantly and developed a covering element like the dome so functionally, that its cupola architecture became unique.

The Turks were originally a Central Asian nomadic people who shepherded on vast plains. Droughts that lasted for hundreds of years and the unfriendly central asian climate compelled them to emigrate to the west in order to find new areas for settlement. They began to settle on Anatolian soil beginning with the 11th century. They became sedentary first during the Great Seljuk Empire and then the Anatolian Seljuk State and gradually turned into an agricultural society which set on to create its own architecture.

In the beginning, Seljuk architecture was a typical imitation and synthesis of many other styles and its outstanding performance made itself visible in monumental portals. The Seljuks copied other styles and used Georgian, Armenian, Arabian, Roman and Byzantine ele-

ments in decorating their portals, creating a very fine and extraordinary stone work. But the deaf and mute walls of the Seljuk Turks never reveal the function of the building from the outside: It is quite difficult to differentiate between a Seljuk mosque and caravansary when we look at it from a distance. Only the minarets can give a clue. The Seljuks also used the cupola as a covering element but the " young" Seljuk architecture could not add a shaking splendor to it yet. They mostly constructed buildings with many domes, columns and nevas.

Ottoman architecture, on the other hand, underlined the importance of the big central dome as it is seen in the splendid examples built in Bursa and Edirne in the 15th century. Dome architecture reached its peak in the mosques of İstanbul that were built in the city after the conquest.

The first mosque built after 1453 is the Fatih mosque and it heralds this new architectural concept. The " külliye" complex which was composed of elementary and high schools, a hospital, a soup kitchen, libraries, an orphanage and residences for the elderly was a huge religious, educational and social complex with a grand mosque at its center. Its architectural style developed in time. The " külliye" architecture reached its peak in the second half of the 16th century with the Turkish-Ottoman architect Grand Sinan who was undoubtedly the most productive and the best artist of the Ottoman times. The Süleymaniye

mosque and its " külliye" in İstanbul and especially the Selimiye mosque with its " külliye" in Edirne are only two of the masterpieces where his contribution to the art of architecture are clearly seen.

The Harem and the Justice Pavilion.

The period of stagnation which began in the 17th century and the decline of the empire following it have also had an impact on the architecture. Because of economic shortages, the state and the court refrained from constructing gigantic mosques and " külliyes" like they did in the 16th and the 17th centuries. They chose to construct smaller buildings but concentrated more on the decoration, which meant the adoption of yet a different style. The Dolmabahçe and Beylerbeyi Palaces, the summer residences and the small " chalets" along the Bosphorus or in hunting areas are the best examples of that elaborate

style. That style was applied to such buildings of civilian architecture as mosques, small palaces, and "külliye" complexes which were erected by the nobility. But at the same time, houses, chalets and villas at the shores of the Bosphorus were built by other city dwellers who chose cedar wood as a main construction element. The wooden house architecture can also be seen today in the Soğukçeşme street which lies between the Topkapı Palace and the Ayasofya Museum. The most outstanding examples of this kind of housing are the villas which decorate the shores of the Bosphorus. Another exemplary place is the district with the Chora Museum at its center. The Ottoman wooden houses in both the Soğukçeşme street and around the Chora Museum have been restored by the Turkish Touring and Automobile Institution.

Thousands of such wooden houses in the old districts of İstanbul like Edirnekapı, Kadırga, Çarşamba, Üsküdar, Fener, Kasımpaşa, Eyüp, Karagümrük, Süleymaniye and Balat try to resist the destructive power of time and negligence. The limited economic resources of such a still developing country as Turkey disable their large scale restoration. Natural causes and arson practiced by people looking for building grounds are the biggest enemies of the wooden houses almost every year. Ottoman wooden architecture is a very original style and beauty which should be enjoyed by foreign guests.

In visiting an Ottoman mosque, one should never forget that one of the most important features of almost all these monuments is their identity as part of a religious complex. These "complexes" consist of a great architectural whole in which the mosque, usually located in the center, is surrounded by a number of subsidiary buildings, such as primary schools, "medreses" or theological colleges, hospitals, libraries and soup-kitchens for the poor. A characteristic feature of these complexes is a certain modesty of approach in which the main stress is laid on function, with an avoidance of all unnecessary decoration and with windows large enough to provide adequate illumination but small enough to allow the building to be easily heated on the coldest winter day. These buildings are filled with a mystical peace and tranquillity that inspires relaxation and repose, together with a quiet nostalgia that takes one back to centuries long past. Many people of quite different beliefs, or without any beliefs at all, have found peace and harmony in the interiors of these mosques or in strolling through the gardens surrounding them and have plunged into meditation, attaining true tranquillity in an enrichment of the soul. The cemeteries which can be seen in all these mosques as well as in combination with almost all examples of Ottoman secular architecture are filled with tombstones of the most extraordinary refinement and elegance which serve to impress upon the spectator the shortness and transitoriness of human life.

Indeed, their primary function would appear to have been to remind us of the vanity of all wordly desires and ambitions. These cemeteries, shaded by ancient trees planted centuries ago, carry us away from normal reality into quite another, mysterious world. By keeping all this in mind while wandering through these Ottoman mosques we shall be better able to appreciate their architectural magnificence and the important place they occupy in the history of architecture. Sinan and all the other architects of the 15th –17th centuries, in which Ottoman architecture reached the peak of its achievement, laid particular stress not only on skill but also on a

Views from Soğukçeşme Street.

certain sense of strength and power. That is why all the mosques created during this period, from the greatest to the smallest, are dominated by the one main motif of "strength, power and magnificence". These mosques, with their restrained decoration and a taste characterised by a certain element of self-confidence, are all symbols of imperial greatness and power. The mosques created in the period of stagnation and decline that began in the 18th century are distinguished by a greater delicacy, a greater refinement and a rather greater maturity, but are, at the same time, accompanied by a certain sense of fatigue and weariness. The huge monuments and "complexes" of the previous period are now replaced by buildings displaying a detailed refinement that penetrates into the innermost corners of the building. The bigotry and religious fanaticism that formed what was perhaps one of the main distinguishing features of political and social decline manifests itself in architecture in the weakening of the Turkish element and its replacement by arabesque. And yet, to whatever century they may belong, all these mosques survive as examples of a quite incredible beauty and visual splendor amidst the horrors of a 20th century concrete civilization that has flooded the whole city with the most revolting tastelessness and ugliness

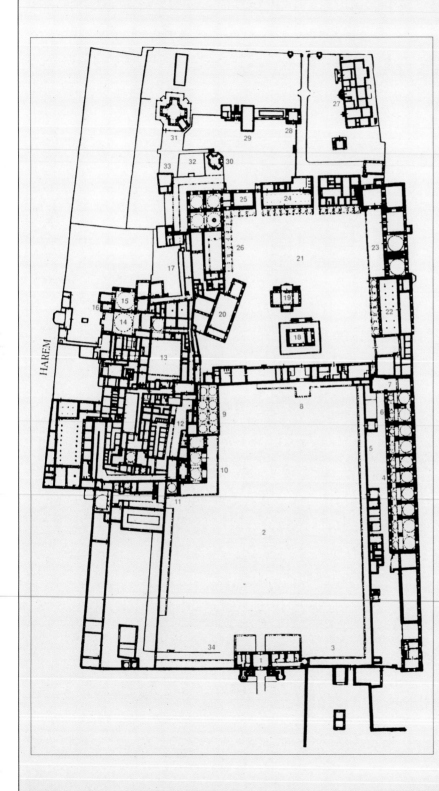

PLAN OF TOPKAPI PALACE

1 - Main gate (Babü's Selam)
2 - The 2nd courtyard
3 - Chariots Section
4 - Chinese and Japanese porcelain Section
5 - The European Porcelain Section
6 - Palace Kitchenware Section (helvahane)
7 - Istanbul Glassware and Porcelain Section
8 - The Akağalar Gate
9 - The Weapons Section
10 - The Kubbealtı
11 - Entrance to the Harem
12 - The Courtyard of the Karaağalar
13 - The Courtyard of the Valide Sultan
14 - The Hünkâr Sofası
15 - The Room of Sultan Murat III.
16 - The Fruit Room
17 - The Courtyard of the Favorites
18 - Audience Chamber
19 - Library of Ahmed III.
20 - The Library (Ağalar Mosque)
21 - The 3rd courtyard
22 - Textiles and Kaftans Section
23 - The Treasury section
24 - The Inscriptions, Miniatures and Sultans Portraits Section
25 - The Clocks Section
26 - The Sacred Relics Section
27 - The Mecidiye Pavilion
28 - Hekimbaşı Tower
29 - The Sofa Pavilion
30 - The Revan Pavilion
31 - The Bagdat Pavilion
32 - Pool
33 - The Circumcision Room
34 - The Bookstore

Topkapı Palace

Topkapı Palace.

For nearly 400 years, Topkapı Palace served both as a residence for 24 Ottoman Sultans, their entourage and their servants, as well as the administrative center of the Ottoman State. Today, it remains as an outstanding and magnificent example of Ottoman secular architecture and as one of the largest palace museums in the world, with a rich collection of some 86,000 items.

After Sultan Mehmet II conquered Istanbul in 1453, he settled in a small palace he had erected on the site of today's Istanbul University. The Sultan and his family lived in this palace for a long time. The construction of a new palace began on the commanding point of the peninsula on which the old city perched in either 1465 or 1470, depending on the historical source referred to. Together with the start of this construction, the palace that the Sultan resided in began to be known as the 'Old Palace', while that under construction was to be known as the 'New Palace.' It was the mid-19th century before the New Palace was to be referred to as the 'Topkapı Palace, whereas until then it was always known as the 'New Palace' or simply the 'Palace.

The palace occupies a triangular site of 700,000 m_ at the point of confluence of the Bosphorus, the Golden Horn and the Sea of

Marmara, which formed the earliest known place of settlement in the European section of Istanbul. The walls surrounding the palace are five kilometers in length and have seven great entrance gates, four on the landward side and three towards the sea. Work on the construction of the palace began in 1470 but modifications and additions continued to be made until 1850, when the building assumed its final shape. The name Topkapı, or Cannon Gate, is derived from the name of the gate at Seraglio Point.

Fountain of Ahmet III.

During the Byzantine period, there were green fields and olive groves on the wide clearing where the Palace is situated. Today, when conducting an archaeological study of the building materials that comprised of the palace foundations, and evaluating it along with some data noted by Byzantine historians, we have learned that there were a couple of pagan temples on this site in ancient times, whereas these temples were subsequently torn down and two or three churches were erected in their place. These small churches were removed during the construction of the palace.

The inner palace is situated on a hill 50 meters above sea-level and covers an area of 220 x 370 m. The main entrance, the 'Bab-ı Hümayun' or Imperial Gate, is located just behind Ayasofya. This gate was built during the reign of Sultan Mehmet II and bears an inscription with the date 1478. It was the scene of a number of important ceremonies and events. The palace consists of a series of courtyards opening one into the other, surrounded by mostly one-storey buildings.

When you go around the Ayasofya Museum and proceed to the palace walls and the Sultan's Court, you will see the Soğukçeşme street extending between the castle walls and the back side of Ayasofya. The beautiful wooden houses cited above are here. If you face the palace portal, you will also see a monumental fountain called the Fountain of Ahmet III. Its very fine stone work and beautiful tiles undoubtedly make it the prettiest monumental fountain of the Ottoman Age.

When the sultans resided in the Topkapı Palace, foreign visitors had to stop at this portal and wait to be accepted inside. In the meantime, they washed at the Fountain of Ahmet III and tended their looks. The beauty and splendor of this monument were there to impress the visitor and to crush him with the grandeur of the sultan and the state.

I. The First Court (Alay Meydanı - Court of Processions)
II. Bab-üs Selam (Gate of Salutation)
III. Second Court (Divan Meydanı - Court of the Imperial Council)
IV. Bab-üs Saade (Gate of Felicity)
V. Fourth Court (Tulip Garden and Sofa)

The First Court

The First Court is 300 meters in length. On the right stood the timber stores, hospital, bakeries, greenhouses and armories. Of the 12 pavilions constructed at various times in the First Court and in the area extending down to the sea on the right, only the Çinili Köşk (Tiled Pavilion), the Alay Köşkü (Review Pavilion) and the Sepetçiler Köşkü (Basketmaker's Pavilion) are still standing. The First Court came to be known as the "Alay Meydanı" or Court of Processions, because of the military, bayram and funeral ceremonies which were held there. From time to time, javelin throwing contests, wrestling matches or other sportive events were held in this wide court. It was also used as a training grounds for the thousands of soldiers who who held responsible for palace security.

On the left-hand side of the courtyard stands the Church of Hagia Eirene. Formerly used as an armory, this church, which measures 32 x

The Imperial Gate.

100 meters, was built by Emperor Justinian in 537. The only church in Istanbul not to have been converted into a mosque after the conquest of the city by the Turks, it is now used as a venue for exhibitions and concerts. With its original architecture, intriguing structure and astounding acoustics, it is one of the most beautiful churches of the Byzantine period. The building, which had suffered damaged from various earthquakes and fires, was always restored and renovated in accordance with the original plan. One can make out the pale wall fragments remaining from the time when the Hagia Eirene was first erected as those closest to the foundation.

Having lost its congregation due to the fact that its Christian followers living in neighborhoods in the vicinity of the city's Palace were evicted to other neighborhoods, the Hagia Eirene was utilized for some time as the Palace arsenal and armory.

Built right next to the church and over the slope of the cliff and immediately behind it was the Imperial Mint, which continued operations from 1665 to 1967 and at one time employed as many as 400

guildsmen. On the first day of each month the Director of the Mint would deliver to the palace 10,000 freshly minted gold sovereigns and 20,000 silver coins.

Set against the wall in the right-hand corner of the First Court at a distance of 25 meters from the second gate stands the Executioner's Fountain where those condemned to death by the Sultan were beheaded. The head was then placed on the Ibret Taşı (Admonition Stone) immediately beside the fountain, where it was left for some time on public display as a warning to others. The fountain was given the name Executioner's Fountain as it was here that the executioner washed the blood from his hands and weapon.

The First Court was also known as the Janissary Court as it was here that the Janissaries assembled when on duty in the palace. Most of the Janissary revolts, which occurred frequently in the Empire's period of decline, would start in this courtyard and expand. In particular, starting in the 18th century, the Janissaries who by then had began to go astray from their disciplined ranks and resisted some decisions of the state administration, would commence their mutinies here with a ceremony known as "upturning the rice kettles." Because they didn't

Front :
Hagia İrene.

Back :
General view of the
Palace.

A miniature of
Topkapı Palace,
XVIII cent.

have any other soldiers to use against the Janissaries, the Sultans were forced to sacrifice their Pashas or Veziers and would have them executed.

These revolts would go further than this and would end with the dethroning of the Sultan. In a worse case instance, the Janissaries weren't satisfied with knocking Osman the Young off his throne, they threw a noose over his neck, carried him off to the Yediküle Dungeons and tortured him to death.

Hagia Irene.

Bab-üs Selam
(Gate of Salutation)

The gate opening into the Second Court now serves as the entrance to the museum. Only the Sultan entered this gate on horseback, and even the Grand Vizier and other viziers were obliged to dismount at this point and enter the palace on foot. Built by Sultan Mehmet the Conqueror, it was formerly known as the Gate of Salutation because it was on the "salutation stones" in this courtyard that the members of the court would greet the Grand Vizier on his way to the Council of State. It is also known as the Orta Kapı or Central Gate because of its location in the center of the palace. The inscription on the left-hand side of the gate refers to its repair by Sultan Süleyman the Magnificent in 1525. The large inscription over the outer gate consists of a Kelime-i Şehadet (confession of faith - there is one God and Muhammed is His Prophet) and the Kelime-i Fevhid (the declaration of God's unity). The two octagonal conical towers of hewn stone flanking the gate were built by Süleyman the Magnificent in 1525. Between the two gates

*View from the Gate
of Salutation.*

there is a fountain erected in 1758, while on the inner side of the gate
there is a portico with ten columns and wide eaves constructed by
Mustafa III (1757-1789). The towers in the inner section of the gates
contained the quarters of the Gate Ağa and the gate keepers, and it
was here that foreign dignitaries to the palace would wait for permis-
sion to enter. The gate also contained the quarters of the head executioner and the cells in which the condemned awaited execution. The
gate exhibited two very different appearances from the outside and
inside. From the first courtyard, that is, when looking from outside, it
conveys the look of a castle gate, one that carries the features of military architecture. Whereas, looking at it from the inside, that is, from
the First Courtyard, one is presented with a grand pavilion adorned
with very wide and rich ceiling decorations. This place, which is decorated with incredible examples of calligraphy, is one of the most beautiful spots of the Topkapı Palace.

The Second Court

The Second Court is in the form of a rectangle measuring 130 x 160 meters and covering a total area of 20,800 m2. Built mainly during the reign of Mehmet the Conqueror, it still preserves much of its original form. The court contains a number of fountains, the Beşirağa Mosque, the palace stables, the Mehterhane (quarters of the mehter, or military band), the Zülüflü Baltacılar Koğuşu (quarters of the Halberdiers with Tresses), Ottoman stone inscriptions, the Old Treasury (which now houses the weapon collection) and a Byzantine cistern, while beside the second gate on the right can be seen the namazgâh (open-air place of worship), the pantries, the granary, the Ahçılar Mosque, the palace kitchens, the mesjid of the "şekerciler" or confectioners and the quarters of the cooks.

A number of cedar trees are situated along the path that stretches between the two gates as well as in the exact center of the courtyard. A fig tree and a juniper tree have taken root in the trunks of two cedars found along the left side of the path. Having one type of tree growing within the trunk of another type is a rather rare occurence. Also to be found in this courtyard are great plane trees hundreds of years old.

Above :
Colonnades of the
second courtyard,

Below :
Views from the
second courtyard.

The Second Court is known as the Divan Meydanı or Council Court. 'Divan' was the name given to the government of the Ottoman State, that is, the Council of Ministers. At times when the Sultan wasn't present, this council which was comprised of Viziers or Ministers, would assemble with the Grand Vizier as Chairman. Though he didn't have the title of Vizier, the Şeyhülislam, who was second on the religious totem-pole behind the Sultan who was also the Caliph, was a natural member of this board.

Again, though they didn't possess the title of Vizier, the Governor-Generals of Anatolia and Rumelia would participate in the Council whenever they were in Istanbul. The Second Court was the part of the palace where this Divan (Council of State) met four times a week. When the Council was in session, state employees, palace guards and Janissaries, numbering 5,000 on ordinary days and 10,000 on special days, would assemble in this court and wait in absolute silence.

The Kubbealtı, or Council Chamber, constructed by the architect Sinan on the left-hand side of the Divan

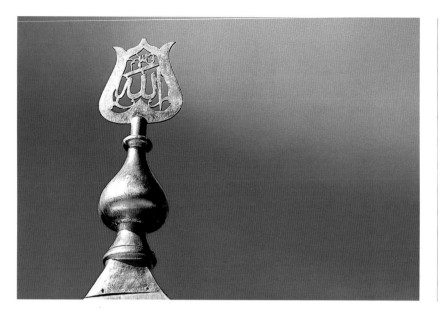

Above :
The standard of a
dome

Below :
The second
courtyard and the
chimneys of the
kitchen.

Court, consists of three rooms roofed by three domes and with broad eaves in front. The building suffered a great deal of damage from fire, and there are inscriptions giving information regarding the repairs carried out on those occasions.

In earlier times the meetings of the Council of State were attended by the Sultan in person, but from the reign of Süleyman the Magnificent onwards it became the custom for the Sultan to follow the debates conducted in Council from a latticed window immediately above the seat occupied by the Grand Vizier.

This window has a rather interesting function. In the Ottoman empire, the sultan had full authority on the lives of the viziers until the Tanzimat Restoration in 1839. The sultan could order the decapitation of a vizier in a moment of anger and he could not be held responsible for his decision. Thus, the viziers who were the equivalents of today's ministers had to be very careful in speech and deed. Ottoman history is full of decapitated viziers and grand viziers.

The latticework of the window mentioned above was constructed

Views from the second courtyard.

39

so intensely, that no one in the assembly hall could ever tell whether the sultan was behind it or not. All the viziers had to be very careful and serious during the meetings. After the session was over, the grand vizier, that is the prime minister, went to the Audition Room through the Door of Happiness (Bab-üs Saade) to convey the whole meeting to the sultan and answer his questions.

Since he couldn't know of the sultan's possible presence behind the window, he took care to tell him all the details fully and correctly. Any mistake could cost him his life. This clever and witty detail enabled the sultans to leave the matters of the state to their ministers, to be sure of their accurateness, and to have all the free time to enjoy their concubines.

Meals were sometimes served here to the Viziers and ambassadors.

The interior is in the Baroque style with tile decoration. The Adalet Kulesi (Justice Tower) immediately beside it rises to a height of 45 meters.

On the right-hand side of the Second Court can be seen the many domes and chimneys of the palace kitchens. Repaired in 1945, these now house an extremely valuable collection of porcelain. It was in these kitchens, 150 meters in length, that meals were prepared each day for the 3,000 palace staff and soldiers. Every day, fresh fruit and

The second courtyard and the chimneys of the kitchen.

vegetables were delivered to the palace kitchens, together with 200 sheep, 100 lambs, 40 calves and 40 geese and ducks, while in the autumn this would be supplemented by "pastırma" (a pressed meat cured with garlic and other spices) from 400 cattle. Every year saw the delivery of 20,000 hens and 2,000 turkeys. Rice, sugar, chickpeas and saffron were brought from Egypt, honey and candle-wax from Thrace and salt from the Salt Lake (Tuz Gölü). In summer 880 camel-loads of ice was brought from Uludağ. All this material was cooked by 400 cooks divided into seven groups.

Today, the kitchens house the richest collection of Chinese porcelain in the world after Beijing and Dresden, with 4,584 items on display selected from a total collection of 10,512.

The first six rooms contain a collection of porcelain ranging from Celadon ware dating from the Sung dynasty (960-1368) to the 18th century Ming dynasty, while the seventh room houses an exhibition of Japanese porcelain.

The use of Chinese porcelain in the palace

began during the reigns of Mehmet II (1451-1481) and Bayezıd II (1481-1512) and was continued by Selim I (1512-1520), who is said to have brought back Chinese porcelain from the palace of Shah Ismail in Tabriz, and by Süleyman the Magnificent, who showed a great interest in blue-and-white porcelain.

The porcelain collection was gradually augmented by gifts to the Sultan from foreign potentates, purchase, booty and the acquisition or confiscation by the palace of the property of deceased or dismissed court dignitaries. The most curious of the porcelain objects displayed is the Celadon ware, which is supposed to change color if poison is present in the food. Celadon ware owes its light green color to the use of iron oxide.

To pass into the section where the kitchens are, one can pass through two of the three existing passageways, the third one of which is closed. These passageways are visible imediately after entering into the second courtyard and turning right. If one passes through the one on the right, one enters an exhibit comprised of seven consecutive halls where the Celadon and Chinese porcelain ware is found.

It is recommended to follow this exhibit from a chronological standpoint, whereas one will first encounter the pale green Celadon ware and pieces crafted during the succeeding centuries, the blue-whites and finally the multi-colored porcelain ware.

While wandering through this carousel of color and beauty, we

On the right, above:
Hırka-i Saadet.

On the right, below:
Kubbealtı

Below :
Justice or Sultan's pavilion.

would like to draw your attention by having you look up at the ceiling every so often and admire the very interesting architecture of the building, which is a work of the great architect Sinan.

Justice or Sultan's pavilion.

Copper Kitchen Utensils

Interior views from the kitchens.

Towards the end of the corridor and right next to the halls where the porcelain collections are found is where the final hall of the kitchens is located. This hall used to be called the "Helvahane." Various helva, desserts and syrups, which made up a very rich part of the Turkish-Ottoman cuisine, were prepared here. Today, this section is used to exhibit the kitchen utensils.

The Helvahane (Confectionery) section of the palace kitchens contains a collection of copper pans and cauldrons, dishes with lids, "sefertas" (food boxes with several metal dishes fastened together) and rose-water flasks. The copper cauldrons, some of them 60-70 centimeters in diameter, were used for making "helva", a sweet prepared from sesame oil, various cereals and syrup or honey, and in the preparation of "macun", a sort of toffee made from 41 different spices and distributed every year to the inmates of the palace at the Nevruz Festival.

The food dishes with lids are made of either copper or brass. One of these, dated 1824, belonged to the wife of Sultan Mahmut II (1808-1839), and there are also dishes belonging to Behice Sultan, the daughter of Sultan Abdülmecit (1839-1861). A section of the kettles, trays and shallow frying-pans that are on display here have original Turkish dec-

orative motifs on them. The copper kettles and trays were crafts using a coppersmith technique called martelé, which is particular to the Turkish art of coppersmithing.

Ewers employed in washing hands and in ritual ablutions, salep, sherbet and milk jugs, braziers, trays for böreks and sweets, censers for the incense burned after meals and rose water flasks are also to be found in this section.

Ottoman Silver and European Crystal

The building opposite the palace kitchens on the right-hand side of the Second Court formerly allotted to the palace servants now houses a collection of Ottoman Silver and European Crystal comprising silver vases, writing sets, pen sets, sweet sets, "karlıks" (glass vessels with two compartments, one of which is filled with snow, for cooling liquids) braziers, coffee pots, bird cages, samovars, tea sets and models, such as a model of the Ahmet III Fountain.

The narrow and long building where these items are exhibited is located between the kitchens and the Second Court, whereas the passageways used to enter the kitchens are found under this building. These works, which are displayed in this building, the entrance of which is through the corridor on the kitchen side, belong mostly to the 18th and 19th centuries. Gifts which were presented to Sultans to celebrate their anniversaries of ascension to the throne reflect special attention.

Istanbul Glass and Porcelain

There is a small building at the upper end of this interesting, narrow corridor which is to be used as a mescit by the kitchen personnel. Today, the "sherbet" section of the palace kitchens in the Second Court houses a collection of 900 items of Beykoz, Paşabahçe and Yıldız glass and porcelain ware which was produced in Istanbul beginning in the 19th century. The first porcelain factory in Istanbul was opened at Beykoz in 1845 and the second at Yıldız Palace in 1894. Experts were brought to Yıldız from the Sévres factory in France and many of the items produced here were specially prepared for the palace itself. This section contains various examples of Yıldız porcelain, such as wall panels, boxes, plates and cups, together with Beykoz cups, white and colored Beykoz ware and Paşabahçe lamps and other glassware.

Two of Palace porcelains.

Arms Museum

Some 400 items from a collection of over 10,000 weapons are displayed in the old Treasury building, which is an extension of the Kubbealtı where the Ottoman Cabinet assembled in the Second Court. This collection comprises of maces, lances, swords, daggers, yataghans, bows and arrows, fire-arms, chain mail and armor, helmets and shields dating from the 7th-20th centuries. The Ottoman palace contained a collection of weapons belonging to the sultans and the viziers, various weapons presented as gifts or siezed as booty and a number of weapons adorned with precious stones. Other weapons were stored in the armory in Hagia Eirene, whence they were subsequently transferred to the Arms Museum. A collection of Ottoman, Arab, Mamluke and Persian weapons was thus built up in the palace itself. The oldest swords are those belonging to the Umayyad and Abbasid Caliphs, ranging from the period of the Prophet Muhammed to the 13th century, brought to Istanbul by Selim I in 1517. The lances belonging to the 15th century Mamlukes are very heavy iron weapons with long points, the Turkish lances are made of reed or hard wood with points with smooth or milled edges, while the Persian lances are of reed or hard wood with fine, forked or pointed ends.

The Persian swords of the 17th and 18th centuries are curved with very sharp points. The collection also contains Crimean and Caucasian swords of the 17th and 18th centuries.

The central showcase contains various Turkish, Persian and Mamluke accesories such as helmets, standards, shields, maces, axes, armour and quivers.

The collection also contains rifles, pistols and swords of the 17th –20th centuries, as well as the Japanese sword and armor presented to Sultan Abdülhamid II in 1891. There are also decorated swords belonging to 15 Ottoman sultans.

The Harem

The term "harem" is used to refer to the private rooms in a Muslim house. The Harem section of Topkapı Palace consisted of the private apartments on the left hand side of the Second and Third Courts in which accommodation was provided for the Ottoman Sultans and their families. It was originally built by the architect Sinan for Murat III in 1578, but after being completely burned down in 1665 it gradually assumed the form we find it in today by the addition of a number of wooden rooms and pavilions built by Mehmed

Ornementations from the Harem.

IV in 1665-1668, Osman III in 1756, Abdülhamit I in 1779 and Selim III in 1789, giving rise to an extremely complicated, labyrinth plan. As the first Ottoman Sultans were almost continually on campaign most of their time was spent outside the Harem, but from Selim III onwards Sultans rarely left the palace. The imperial family, comprising the Sultan himself, his mother, his wives, his children and his concubines, lived in a part of the palace completely closed to the outside world and even to other parts of the palace complex. The Harem was absolutely impenetrable, with thick, high walls guarded by the Harem Ağas, or Black Eunuchs. The Harem constituted a city in itself, covering an area of 13,000 m_, containing 400 rooms and courtyards and housing 1,200 people, including the servants. The Harem Ağas, who were responsible for the security and other services of the Harem and sections

Inner gate of the Harem.

51

belonging to the Sultan and his family, were divided in two groups, according to their race and skin color, the Ak Ağas (White Eunuchs) and the Kara Ağas (Black Eunuchs). While the Kara Ağas dealt only with the Harem, that is, the section where the women were, the Ak Ağas were responsible for the security and services of the Third Court, where the Sultan's private garden was located, and beyond. This is why the passage gate into the Third Court was known as the "White Eunuchs' Gate."

The common feature of these Harem Ağas was the fact that they were all eunuchs. Generally, they were prisoners who were captured during wars or else the young of those slaves presented to the palace were chosen and castrated through an operation carried out be doctors. Women and girls who arrived at the palace were also acquired through various means. These would come from very different ethnic groups. Again they could have been slaves captured in war or else gifts who were presented to the palace. But other than these, slave girls would be sold at slave markets that existed during the 16th and 17th centuries, the wealthiest times of the Empire. To the contrary of what might have been surmised, the number of Western European women who entered the palace in this manner was quite low. They generally weren*t preferred by the Palace as they were returned to

Views from the Harem.

their families who paid ransom. Those girls whose families couldn't pay the ransom demanded were thusly acquired into the Harem.

The most important criteria for entering the Harem was the age of the girls. Taking into consideration the fact that older girls weren't able to respond properly to the training or else were having difficulty, younger girls were always the preference.

Views from the Harem.

The concubines, who could be of Turkish, Circassian, Georgian or foreign origin, were taught handicrafts, music and deportment. The more beautiful and talented had hopes of becoming a wife of the Sultan. The concubines were allowed to leave the palace after serving for nine years, and some of them, on retirement, married high-ranking court dignitaries. The most beautiful concubines, who were chosen for special service to the Sultan, were known as "odalisques," while a concubine who bore the Sultan a son was given the title "Haseki." The Sultans Mustafa I and

Osman III showed no interest whatsoever in the concubines, and in order to avoid them altogether Osman III had nails attached to the soles of his shoes so that the concubines would hear him approach and make themselves scarce.

The Harem apartments were adorned with tiles, wood carving and pictures. Today's entrance to the Harem is to be found immediately

Views from the Harem.

beside the Carriage Gate (Araba Kapısı). This gate is to the immediate
of the Kübbealtı, where the Ottoman Cabinet would assembly. Visitors
wishing to wander through the Harem need to pass through the Bab-
üs Selam Gate, which is the
entrance gate to the museum,
and into the Second Court.
They would then arrive in
front of the Kübbealtı, which
is situated on the path to the
left, perpendicular to the one
running through the middle
of the court. Visitors turning
left will come in front of the
Harem entrance, which is a
second museum inside the
museum, which is subject to
a separate entrance fee. It
was through this gate, erected by Murat III in 1588, that
the ladies would enter and
leave the Harem by carriage.

*Fountains of the
Harem.*

The gate leads to the Dolaplı Kubbe (Dome with Cupboards), so called because of the cupboards in which the Black Eunuchs stored their documents. This section was repaired in 1733. From the Dolaplı Kubbe we enter the Şadırvanlı Sofa (the chamber with the shadirvan). This was the guard-post of the Kara Harem Ağas or Black Eunuchs. Here, too, are to be found the Mosque of the Black Eunuchs and a watch tower. The chamber itself, lit by four windows and roofed with a dome, is decorated with 17th century tiles. The upper portion contains the name of God and the 10 people whom the Prophet Muhammed declared would go to heaven (Ebubekir, Ömer, Osman, Ali, Abdurrahman, Ebu Ubeyde, Talha,

Above :
A fountain in the Harem.

Below :
Some stained-glass.

Zübeyr, Said and Sad). Here too is to be found the Sultan's horse block. This block was placed here in order to present an easier means for Sultans who were advanced in years to mount their steeds. It was used particular by Sultans who didn't like to be touched by the Harem Ağas who assisted them in getting onto the horse. The pool to which the Şadırvanlı Sofa owes its name was later transferred to the marble terrace occupied by the apartments of Osman III.

After the Şadırvanlı Sofa comes the Palace Tower, which rises to a height of 45 meters and is the first part of the palace to attract attention from a distance. It was erected by Mehmet IV in 1668 as a watch tower from which the area surrounding the palace could be kept under observation during any possible disturbances. The square, two-storey building with hexagonal conical roof known as the Adalet Kasrı (Justice Pavilion) or Sultan Kasrı (Royal Pavilion) contains a stair of 105 steps leading up to the tower above. The second landing contains the latticed window through which the Sultan followed the meetings in the Council Chamber below. The Karaağlar Mescidi (Mesjid of the Black Eunuchs) on the left of the Şadırvanlı Sofa was built in the 17th century and adorned with tiles dating from the same period. It was in this mesjid that the princes learned the principles of the Koran. A corridor with a portico supported by six columns and tile revetment on the

Views from the Harem.

walls on both right and left leads from the Şadırvanlı Sofa to the Altın Yol (Golden Way). This passage is also known as the Karaağalar Taşlığı (Court of the Black Eunuchs) because of the Mesjid of the Black Eunuchs immediately beside it. On the right stand the quarters of the Musahips who would entertain the Sultan with their conversation and of the dwarfs who would amuse him with their antics, as well as the apartments of the Treasurers (Hazinedar) who were responsible for the various ceremonies and entertainments and for the care of precious luxury objects and the Sultan's seal. At the end of the corridor is the entrance gate to the Harem and the Corridor of the Concubines. At the beginning of the corridor stands the

Above :
The Imperial
Council.

Below :
On the left, a
miniature of
musicians, XVIII
cent.
On the right, the
wall decorations.

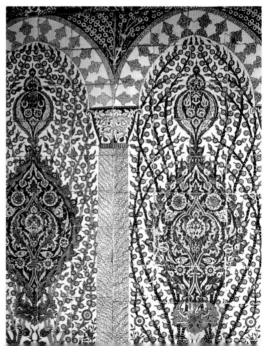

platform on which the food cauldrons were set, while the whole corridor is lined with long marble tables and shelves on which the dishes were placed.

The Karaağalar Koğuşu (Dormitory of the Black Eunuchs) was built in the 17th century. The marble inscription at the entrance informs us that when one of the Harem Ağas retired and was given his freedom it was the custom for three month's salary to be col-

Views from the Harem.

lected from each of the other eunuchs and the whole sum presented to him. The dormitory is a four-storey building containing 22 rooms. The ground floor contains rooms revetted with 17th century tiles. This floor also contains the apartment of the head of the Black Eunuchs.

In front of the entrance to the Harem stands the Kızlar Ağası Dairesi (apartment of the Chief Black Eunuch), a negro of Ethiopian origin with the rank of vizier responsible for the administration of the Harem. His apartment is a two-storey building decorated with 17th century European tiles. He was also responsible for the education of the princes and princesses in the schoolrooms on the floor above. The Kadın Efendiler Taşlığı (the court of the Sultan's Wives) is also known as the Cariyeler Üst Taşlığı (the upper court of the Concubines).

In the same court are to be found the Cariyeler Hamamı (the Baths of the Concubines), the three apartments belonging to the Sultan's wives or "Kadın Efendis", the dormitory of the first concubines, the school of music, the laundry, the kitchens and the pantry. From here there are two stairs, one leading down to the funeral court-yard and the other to the garden. The dormitory of the first concubines is the largest apart-ment in the Harem,

Below :
Sultan's place in the
Imperial Lodge.

Above :
Fruit room of
Ahmet III.

some of the rooms being large enough to accommodate 100 persons. On the tiles in the interior is to be found the inscription "Ey kapıları açan Allah'ım bizlere hayırlı kapılar aç" (Oh God, who opens the doors, open for us the doors of good fortune!). The concubines were the personal property of the Sultan and between 500-700 girls of various races and nationalities were accepted in the Harem to be trained as concubines. It was always possible for a concubine to become one of the wives of the Sultan, or they might marry a court servant or one of their music teachers. Great importance was given to musical education in the palace, and instruction was given in various instruments. A second court, known as the Lower Court, situated 12 meters below the level of the Upper Court of the Concubines, contained the hospital of the concubines, the hospital kitchens, the physician's room, the dormitory of the second concubines, the wood store, the baths, the place of the ablution of the dead, the gate of the dead and the laundry.

Next to the Apartments of the Kadın Efendis are to be found the Apartments of the Valide Sultan, the Mother of the Sultan or Dowager Empress. This section was constructed in 1667 and repaired in 1817. The Valide Sultan held one of the most powerful positions in the Ottoman court and created a female despotism that held the Palace and the Harem under its arbitrary sway. They also had a large body of

Tile decorations in the Harem.

concubines at their disposal. The most famous of the Valide Sultans were Hafsa Sultan, the mother of Süleyman the Magnificent, Hürrem Sultan, the mother of Selim II, Safiye Sultan, the mother of Mehmed III, Kösem Sultan, the mother of Murat IV and Ibrahim the Mad, Mihrişah Sultan, the mother of Selim III, and Bezmialem Sultan, the mother of Abdülmecit. Next to the apartments of the Valide Sultan lies the sultan's bedchamber, and from here one enters the chamber of Selim III.

The Hünkar Hamamı (Imperial Bath), built by the architect Sinan in the 16th century, is the loveliest of all the baths in the Harem. The section with the gilt bronze lattice screen on the left was reserved for the Sultan himself. The bath contains four marble wash basins and six wash places with gilt taps.

From the Imperial Bath one enters the Hünkar Sofası (Imperial Apartment). Built in the 16th century it first of all served as the Sultan's bedchamber but after the repairs and modifications carried out by Osman III in 1756 the room began to be used for official ceremonies. It is the largest and the most beautiful room in the Harem with a large dome, seven doors, three fountains, a chamber for musical instruments and a musician's balcony. The Valide Sultan, the wives of the Sultan, concubines and favorites would recline on the divans beneath the balcony. The armchairs in this room were gifts from the German Emperor

Wilhelm II and the large clock a gift from Queen Victoria.

From the Hünkar Sofası one passes to the Murat Köşkü (Murat Pavilion), constructed by the architect Sinan in 1578 as the bedroom of Sultan Murat III. This contains two large seating alcoves with carving and gold gilt decoration in the corners, a hearth and a fountain with a number of spouts. The walls are sheathed in Iznik tiles. The Hünkâr Sofası opens into the study of Ahmet I, built in 1608 and repaired in 1705. From here a door leads into a dining room decorated with pictures of fruit dating from 1705.

The Şehzadeler Dairesi (apartment of the Princes) and the Mehmet IV Kasrı (Pavilion of Mehmet IV), built by Mehmet IV in the 17th century and also known as the Çifte Kasırlar (Twin Pavilions), have walls revetted with tiles and are served by a single door. It was here that, after finishing their schooling, the princes continued their education with the study of poetry, calligraphy and music. Until the reign of Ahmet I the şehzades would be sent, together with their mothers, as governors of the provinces in order to learn the art of administration, but from the reign of that Sultan onwards they never left the Harem, spending all their time confined to these rooms. This section of the Harem also contained the Çeşmeli Sofa (the room with the Fountain); the Ocaklı Sofa (the room with the hearth), an apartment occupied by the first wife of the Sultan which derived its name from the hearth at which the brasiers were lit and thence distibuted throughout the Harem; the Haseki Dairesi, where concubines were taken to give birth

A view from the Harem.

Moonlight in the Imperial Lodge.

to their children, and a store for valuables. The Altın Yol (Golden Way) was a corridor 45 meters in length forming one of the oldest parts of the Harem, the name Golden Way deriving from the custom performed by the Veliaht Şehzade (Crown Prince) on the day of his accession to the throne of scattering gold coins to the concubines lined up on each side as he passed along the corridor towards the Third Court.

The mysterious Harem which was fully closed to the outer world has always been the most attractive place to trigger the curiosity of many a researcher. The unknown life of the Harem has been the inspiration for many musicians, artists and authors. Their attitudes were usually fictitious since they mostly had to imagine what was going on in there. Though it was dainty and rich, life in the Harem was slavery in the true sense of the word, and it is not possible to conclude that the women were happy with their situation. The young girls who had become members of the Harem were told continuously, that it was their fate to be there, and thus they learned to bow to the authority. Complete and unwavered obedience was the foremost rule, and the sultan mothers ruled the Harem with an iron fist to prevent any possible disorder. Those women who could not put up with that discipline, cried the whole time or refused to be trained were punished merciless-

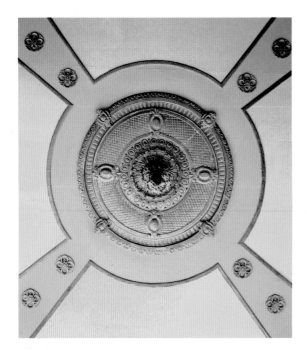

ly. If they still refused to obey the rules, they were put in broadcloth sacks and thrown to the sea at the Seraglio Point.

It is not difficult to guess how difficult and boring Harem life used to be. The women of the Harem could leave their cage only a few times in a year, and when they did so, they either picknicked in the remote gardens of the Golden Horn or made boat tours at the Bosphorus. They must have suffered from inactivity and monotony since there were also hoards of other servants and slaves to do the daily work. Their useless life also incited intrigues, collaborations, hatred, jealousy, suppressed feelings and yearnings, and perversities. It is easy to understand, that the sultan, being the only male in the Harem, could not satisfy all the women whose number reached hundreds from time to time. Consequently, it won't be wrong to call the Harem the " golden cage".

*On the left,
Harem, ceiling
ornementations.*

*On the right,
Tile wall
ornementations.*

The Gate Of Felicity

Bab-üs Saade (Gate of Felicity) is the transition gate into the Third Court of the Palace and resembles the appearance of the Bab-üs Selam Gate from the Second Court, that is, the second entrance gate of the palace and the first entrance into the museum. It is an illuminated and colorful place with a wide and richly decorated pavilion. The Second Court of the palace was where most of the contact with the world outside the Puluce was conducted. As it was the Council assembly Hall, viziers, clerks and other officials would enter and left from here. Nevertheless, as the kitchens were situated here, various foodstuffs would arrive, whereas the merchants who sell them to the palace would wander around here, waiting to be paid. Yet, it was from this third gate, otherwise known as the Gate of Felicity that the number of those able to enter was extremely restricted. The security of this gate belonged to the White Eunuchs. They kept very tight surveillance and would only allow foreign ambassadors who had previously made an appointment to visit, Governors or other high officials who came to call on the Sultan, the Grand Vizier, to inform the Sultan after Council meetings, as well as those who were invited by the Sultan to pass.

The Bab-üs Saade was also variously known as the Ak Ağalar Kapısı (Gate of the White Eunuchs) because of its location immediately beside the quarters of the gate guards, as the Taht Kapısı (Throne Gate) because it was in front of this gate that the throne was placed

The Felicity Gate.

on ceremonial occasions, and as the Arz Kapısı (Gate of Petitions), because of its leading directly to the Imperial Chamber of Petitions. It is fronted by a portico with a single dome and broad eaves resting on four marble columns. It was in front of this gate that, from the reign of Mehmet the Conqueror onwards, the ceremonies held on bayrams or on the Sultan's accession to the throne were held. Funeral ceremonies were also conducted here. The funeral service for the deceased Sultan and the enthronement of the new took place on the same day.

The "ayak divanı" (an emergency meting of the Council of State) was held here on the occasion of Janissary mutinies, when the Janissaries would arrive here after forcing their way through the first and second gates. On only two occasions did they actually pass through the Gate of Felicity itself.

During ceremonies, the Sancak (Standard) was placed on a stone in front of the gate, and it was here, too, that the Sultan handed over the Standard to the Grand Vizier or Pasha who was to represent the Sultan on campaign.

The gate bears a Besmele inscription (Bismillahirrahmanirrahim - In the name of God, the Compassionate, the Merciful) with the tughra of Mahmut II below it and a repair inscription with the date 1775. An inscription written by Ahmet III can be seen on the side of the gate facing the inner court. On each side of the gate there are three large round panels giving the dates of birth and accession to the throne of the Ottoman Sultans.

The Third Court

The Third Court is also known as the Enderun Court after the Enderun school located here. The court covers a square measuring 100 x 100 meters. Immediately opposite the entrance stands the Arz Odası or Chamber of Petitions, to the left the Akağalar Koğuşu (Quarters of the White Eunuchs), the Ağalar Mosque (Library), the Hırka-ı Saadet Dairesi (Pavilion of the Holy Mantle), the Silahtar Koğuşu (Quarters of the Royal Guards) (the Watch and Clock Museum), in the center of the garden the Library of Ahmet III, and on the right the Bab-üs Saade Dairesi, the Enderun School, the Fatih Köşkü (Pavilion of the Conqueror) (the Treasury) and the Hazine Kethüdaları Koğuşu (quarters of the Wardens of the Treasury) (collection of books, calligraphy and royal portraits).

This Third Court, which housed the Enderun, held a very important place in the administration of the Ottoman State, and is the section where Sultans spent a very important part of their daily lives. In other words, it had the true nature of a graduate school that was under the continual observation and supervision of the Sultan. The buildings surrounding the court comprised of the bureaus and dormitories of those connected with the Enderun.

Only the brightest students from the four corners of the Empire could attend this school, and while continuing their education, they were also given different tasks to carry out. They were called "içoğlanları". Only civil servants were brought up here, whereas those graduating from here could not be pressed into military service. Students were divided into four classes. Whether it was during peacetime or war, there were officials who were in the private service of the Sultan. After these, the treasury officials made up another separate group, whereas they were brought up to be the financiers of the future. There was also another group whose job it was to ensure that what the Sultan ate was not tainted. There was one final group which was responsible for the supervision of the Holy Relics. While these Enderun students served here for an indeterminate period, they increased their knowledge by attending theoretical classes and gain experience of daily managerial functions through on-the-job training. Once they were deemed fit, the students would leave the palace after being appointed various tasks.

In short, we wouldn't be mistaken to call the Enderun a sort of "Graduate Business Management Academy."

Chamber of Petitions

Once one passes through this magnificent gate and just opposite it, one encounters a splendid structure on the other side of a corridor which is a few meters wide – the 'Arz Odası' or Chamber of Petitions.

It was in this chamber, originally built by Mehmet the Conqueror, that the Sultan received the Grand Vizier, high state dignitaries and foreign ambassadors, and in which he was given important news. On the right is a fountain erected by Süleyman the Magnificent and repaired by Ahmet III and Mahmut II. Extensive repairs were carried out during the reign of Abdülmecit after the fire of 1856.

The Chamber of Petitions has three doors, two of them opening onto the Gate of Felicity and the third onto the Third Court behind. It is constructed on a rectangular plan measuring 65 m_.

The entrance door is surmounted by a Besmele inscription dated 1724 inscribed by

Library.

Library.

Ahmet III himself. The Throne Room is surrounded by a wide portico with 22 marble columns. The front facade is revetted with marble and 16th century tiles while the interior is roofed with a dome 10 meter in height. The large throne with four feet in the left hand corner was made for Mehmet III in 1596. The lower sections of the throne were damaged in the fire of 1856.

The fountains both inside and outside the Chamber of Petitions were used to prevent the conversations held inside the room from being overheard outside. The same purpose of confidentiality was served by the choice of mutes as attendants.

Foreign ambassadors and their entourage would first be entertained to a meal in the Kubbealtı (Council Chamber), after which the kapıcıbaşıs (ushers) would seize them by both arms and lead them into the Chamber of Petitions. After bowing three times the ambassador would make a speech, which would be followed by a translation. He would then present his letter of credentials and, if he was given a letter in return, would take it in his hand, again bow three times and walk backwards out of the room.

Members of the Council of State could enter the Chamber of Petitions on Sundays and Tuesdays wearing new shoes. On entering the Chamber the Grand Vizier and other high state dignitaries would kiss the hem of the Sultan's robe and take up their position on his right. On leaving, they would kiss the ground in front of the Sultan and retire backwards.

Flask.

The Treasury

The Treasury, which is the most visited section of the Topkapı Palace Museum, evokes much admiration from those who stroll through the four halls where it is housed on the right side of the Third Court, next to the hall containing the Sultans' Garment collection.

The riches on display should not astonish the visitors. One should be reminded that the Ottoman Empire, which spanned three continents, was the world's most powerful state from the mid-15th century,

Topkapı Dagger.

when Istanbul was conquered until the end of the 17th century when Vienna was besieged. Today, there are forty independent nations on territory that used to belong to the Ottomans. Thus, there isn't anything surprising about the palace treasury which is filled the wealth of the Ottomans, who established history's most centralist Empire over such a wide expanse of territory.

It is a known fact that the Ottoman state rapidly receeded starting from the 19th century and was completely bankrupt by the 1850's. Also, the building of luxurious palaces and mansions during this period drove the treasury, which was already in a very difficult position, into dire straits it would never emerge from. In order to stave off oblivion, we know that the State of the Sultans borrowed large sums of money from both western countries and moneylenders based in the Galata district during the final period. However, from a financial standpoint, even in the tightest times, the Ottoman Sultans took great pains to avoid selling off the treasury riches which were their ancestors heritage and heirlooms. Thanks to this conduct, we are able to view the wealth exhibited in these four halls today. What is extremely significant is the fact that despite the recommendation of his closest associates to plunder the Treasury, the last Sultan, Mehmet VI took only his own valuable belongings as he boarded the English warship to abandon his country.

Pendant with ruby.

After the conquest of Istanbul the Ottoman treasury was preserved from 1453 to 1478 in Yedikule (the Castle of the Seven Towers), but after the construction of Topkapı Palace the treasury was transferred first to the building which now houses the weapon collection and then to the four rooms of the Pavilion of the Conqueror in the Third Court. Selim I ordered that after his death his treasury should be sealed, and declared that "if any of my successors should fill this treasury with copper coins the treasury that I have filled with gold sovereigns should be sealed with the seal of that individual and should no longer continue to be sealed with my own." The opening of the treasury took the form of an official ceremony in accordance with this last will and testament. The treasury guards would be lined up on each side of the door. The official in charge of the treasury would bring the key, examine the seal of Selim and open the lock.

Only between 20-30 people could enter the treasury at the same

time. The ceremonial opening and closing of
the treasury is still carried out at the present
day. There was no clear and continuous system
of documentation regarding the acqusition of
valuables in the Ottoman Treasury with the
result that records of only the most valuable
items are preserved in the palace archives.
According to extant documents the objects in
the treasury were acquired in one of the following ways:

I.- Some items consisted of war booty seized
during the campaigns conducted in both East
and West in the 15th – 17th centuries. The most
valuable of such objects were reserved for the
use of the Sultan, after whose death they were
delivered for safekeeping to the official in
charge of the treasury along with other objects
of a personal nature.

II.- There is documentary evidence to the
effect that after the conquest of Istanbul, ambassadors were sent with gifts to Eastern countries
to announce the great event and that letters of
congratulation and a large number of valuable
gifts were received in return.

III.- Some 2,000 craftsmen, including jew-
ellers and furriers, are known to have been
employed in the palace to supply objects to this
treasury, and there is documentary evidence that
a great variety of valuable objects were pro-

Golden pendant.

duced by these craftsmen in accordance with the wishes of the Sultan
and court dignitaries. Moreover, each year for many centuries valuable
objects such as rose-water flasks, censers and gold candlesticks
encrusted with precious stones were carried as gifts to Medina under
the supervision of a representative of the Sultan in the procession
known as the Sürre Alayı. After the capture of Arabia by the British in
World War I the Governor of Medina, Fahrettin Türkkan Pasha,
brought all these gifts back to Istanbul. These were all recorded in the
Medina Register and placed in the Treasury.

IV.- According to Ottoman law, goods belonging to court officials
who had been dismissed from the service were confiscated and placed
in the Treasury. For example, the famous Kaşıkçı Diamond was placed
in the treasury after the execution of Tepedelenli Ali Pasha, Governor
of the Mora.

V.- In the last years of the Ottoman Empire, when closer ties with
Europe had been formed by the visit paid to France by Abdülaziz
(1861-1876) and the friendship with Kaiser Wilhelm II founded by

Abdülhamit II (1876-1909), it became the custom for members of the European royal families to visit the Sultan in Istanbul, bringing with them a number of very valuable gifts which served to further enrich the imperial collection. The treasury exhibits are arranged in four rooms in accordance with the type, material and function of the various items.

The first room contains a laquered leather shield, a pair of silver gilt spurs encrusted with precious stones, ornamented bags for carrying a section of the Koran and a suit of armour belonging to Mustafa II, the ivory inlaid ebony throne used by Murat IV on the Baghdad campaign, rose water flasks and zinc decanters decorated with turquoises and emeralds, Ottoman pistols, arrows and quivers, the sword of Süleyman the Magnificent, various other swords, archery rings, daggers, crystal sweet bowls, cup holders, crystal hookah pipes, a gold

Spoonmaker's diamond.

76

hookah pipe belonging to Mustafa Pasha, the Governor of Van, gold candlesticks belonging to Mehmet Ali Pasha, the Governor of Eygypt, candle snuffers, jade dishes, an ebony walking cane and gold basin and ewer belonging to Abdülhamit II, a model of the palace presented by the Japanese Emperor on the occasion of the 25th anniversary of Abdülhamit II's accession to the throne (1901) and an Indian music box with gold elephants.

The second room contains emeralds and various items decorated with emeralds. Exhibits include the emerald rosary beads of Selim III, chrysolites, emerald earrings, crests and an emerald pendant belonging to Abdülhamit I, an emerald pendant bearing the date 1616 belonging to Ahmet I, the dagger with emerald handle presented to the mother of Mehmet IV on the opening of the Yeni Cami (New Mosque) in 1663, an emerald snuff box, an emerald archery ring, the dagger with three oval emeralds on the side of the handle and a watch at the end which has now become the emblem of Topkapı Palace (this dagger was prepared in 1747 as a gift from Mahmut I to Nadir Shah of Iran, but subsequent to the death of the Shah in a revolt which broke out in Iran the ambassadors returned to Istanbul with the intended gift), a Chinese jade vase with a dragon in relief, a bowl adorned with the Russian imperial double-headed eagle with dark green jade handles presented to Abdülhamit II by the Russian Czar Nicholas II, a jade writing-set, rose-water flasks, a rock crystal water pot and rock crystal candle-sticks

Golden ewerand and mug.

and boxes. The third room contains Sancak Korans, gold Koran caskets, an enamel sweet set belonging to Abdülaziz, a pendant belonging to Mahmut II, diamonds belonging to Ahmet I, gold censers prepared by Hatice Sultan, daughter of Mustafa III, for the tomb of the Prophet and Ottoman and foreign medals ornamented with diamonds, including a miniature of Mahmut II decorated with diamonds. The room also contains the famous 86-carat Kaşıkçı (Spoon-Maker) Diamond. This measures 70 x 60 mm and is surrounded by 49 brilliants arranged in two rows in gold mounts. Little credence, however, should be given to the story that the diamond was found in a rubbish-heap during the reign of Mehmet IV (1648-1687) and exchanged for a set of spoons. It is also said to have formed part of the property belonging to Tepedelenli Ali Pasha confiscated after his execution. The room also contains a gold candlestick adorned with 6,482 brilliants and weighing 48 kilograms made for the tomb of the Prophet. It bears the tughra of Abdülmecit and a date of 1856. The fourth room contains the Persian throne measuring 1.55 x 0.95 x 20 meters presented to Mahmut I by

Music box with elephant, pure gold.

Shah Nadir Shah of Iran in 1747. It has four broad legs in the form of vases, while the back and sides are encrusted with pearls, emeralds, rubies and enamel set in gold mounts. Other exhibits include the hand, skull and various bones allegedly belonging to John the Baptist, a number of belts and buckles, the emerald and turquoise encrusted belt dated 1508 belonging to Shah Ismail of Iran brought back by Selim I from his Persian campaign, the mirror dated 1543 with ebony handle and ivory back belonging to Sultan Süleyman the Magnificent, rock crystal chessmen, a set of crystal belonging to Abdülhamit II, sets of drawers, spoons, prayer-beads, the sword of Osman, the scimitar of Sultan Süleyman the Magnificent, rifles, powder horns and jewel boxes.

Cradle of a crown prince, pure gold.

Palace Clocks and Watches

The Silahtar Koğuşu (Quarters of the Royal Guards) in the Third Court contains a collection of Turkish, German, Austrian, English, French, Swiss and Russian clocks and watches presented to the palace at various times. There are four Turkish clocks dating from the 17th century signed by Bulugat, Şahin, Abdurrahman and Mustafa Aksarayi. The clocks made by Bulugat and Şahin resemble astrolabes.

The oldest of the German clocks dates from the 16th century, the gold Austrian clock decorated with precious stones is dated 1720, while the oldest of the English clocks is signed by Bird and dated 1654. The French pocket watch signed by Breguet with landscapes of the Bosphorus and the Golden Horn and decorated with precious stones was presented by the French Emperor Napoleon Bonaparte to Mahmut II. The Russian table clock with Swiss mechanism was presented by the Russian Czar Nicholas II to Abdülhamit II on the 25th anniversary of his accession.

Costumes of the Sultans

These are exhibited in a room on the right-hand side of the Third Court. The collection includes a cotton caftan and sword, a sleeveless garment and a caftan with gold and silver embroidery on silk worn by Mehmet the Conqueror; a silk, gold embroidered caftan with fur, a short, three-colored silk caftan and a short velvet caftan worn by Sultan Süleyman the Magnificent; an embroidered "bohça" (shawl or wrapper), a head-dress, crest, broad-cloth caftan and a silver embroidered caftan worn by Selim II; a silk caftan and velvet ceremonial caftan worn by Murat III; a silk caftan, a ceremonial caftan and a sleeveless broadcloth caftan with fur lining worn by Ahmet I; a caftan worn by Osman II; a silk, sleeveless robe, a jewelled belt and silk sash worn by Murat IV; a ceremonial caftan with appliqué design belonging to Ibrahim the Mad; a fine silk caftan with tulip design in appliqué, gloves and slippers worn by Süleyman II; a caftan and shalvar worn by Ahmed III; a velvet caftan belonging to the Şehzade Korkut, son of Bayezıd II; the caftan worn by Ahmet I as a child; the caftan and shal-

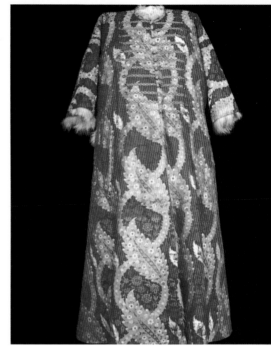

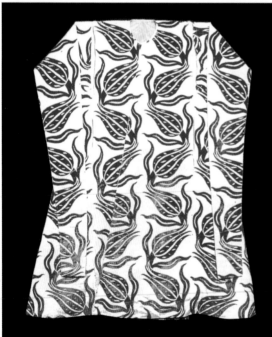

var worn by Mahmut II before the dress reform of 1826 and the trousers, waistcoat and cloak worn after the reform; and the jacket and trouser suit, overcoat, fez and boots worn by Abdülhamit II.

Sultans costumes (kaftans).

Manuscripts, Writing Utensils and the Portraits of the Sultans

Mehmet the "Conquerer".

This collection is housed in the Hazine Kethüdaları (Dormitory of the Treasury Wardens) in the Third Court. The ground floor contains Seljuk Korans in Cufic script, Ilhanid Suras, a Memluke book on horsemanship, a Saffavid copy of the 40 Hadiths, a Koran copied by Sheikh Hamdullah, a calligraphic album belonging to Hafız Osman, a section of the Koran copied by Sultan Abdülmecit, 16th century bindings, binding tools, marbling paper, paper scissors, paper polishes, pen boxes, jewelled inkpot sets, paper knives, and writing sets decorated in ivory, silver or enamel. On the walls are hung pictures, miniatures, cal-

ligraphic panels and tughras. On the upper floor are exhibited large portraits of 36 Ottoman Sultans. Some of these are contemporary. while others were based on information derived from documentary sources.

There are 37 paintings housed in this collection. While some of these are original works painted by foreign artists, some of these works are also copies. For example, the original portrait of Sultan Mehmet the Conqueror, which was painted by Bellini, is found in London's National Gallery. The portrait hanging on these walls is a copy of Bellini's work, which was made by palace artist Zonaro in 1907. The portraits of Orhan Bey and Selim II were also made by

Italian artists. In addition, the portraits of Murat V, by the Russian painter Ayvazovsky, that of Mehmet Reşat by the Austrian artist Krausz as well as that of Abdülaziz, by the Polish artist, Clobowski are also found in this gallery.

Sultan Osman the "Young".

Chamber of the Mantle of the Prophet and Chamber of the Holy Relics

The building in which the holy relics are now housed was built during the reign of Sultan Mehmet the Conqueror. Over the door is the inscription "Essultan Mehmed bin Murad Han" (Sultan Mehmed son of Murat Khan). Square in plan with two large domes, the building closely resembles the Tiled Pavilion, which dates from the same period. The Chamber of the Holy Mantle is entered from the Third Court through the shadirvan door erected during the reign of Ahmet III. Over the door there is a jeli-thuluth Besmele inscription signed by Ahmet III. The door is surrounded with 18th century tiles and two tughras of Ahmet III. It is lit by two spherical lanterns of glass and bronze. The bodies of deceased Ottoman Sultans were washed on the marble platform in front of the door and it was the custom to throw the dust from the Chamber of the Holy Relics into the nearby well.

The Chamber contains priceless relics of the Prophet and other religious leaders brought back by Selim I from Oran, Baghdad, Cairo and Mecca, while other exhibits include items from the Kaaba brought to

Footprint of the prophet.

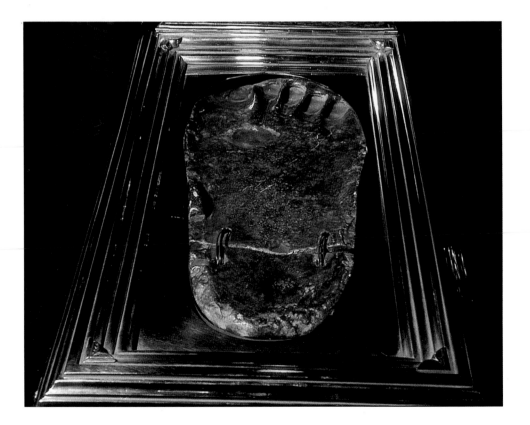

the palace at a later date. Here, in this chamber, during the Ottoman period, throughout the 407 years from 1517 to 1924, 24 "hafız" took turns in a recitation of the Koran that continued without a break for 24-hours a day. The Koran is now recited only during the seven hours a day the museum is open. The Chamber has been open to the public since 31 August 1962. Previously it had been possible to see the relics only by peeping in through the prayer window in the Fourth Court.

On entering from the Third Court one sees the lock and key of the Kaaba which were sent to Istanbul by the Sherif of Mecca after the conquest of Egypt in 1517, together with other locks and keys of the Kaaba inscribed with verses from the Koran and bearing the names of Bayezıd II, Ahmet I and Abdülaziz in silver and gold relief. Here, too,

Golden rim of the Holy Black Stone of Kaaba.

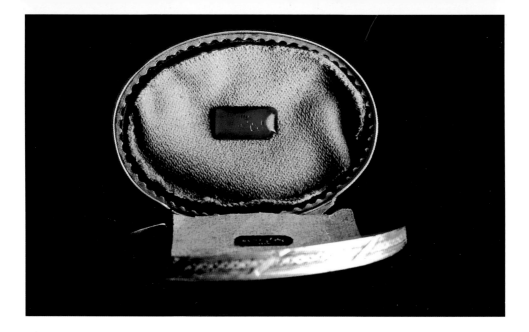

can be seen the sacred sword of the Prophet and swords belonging to the four Caliphs, Ebubekir, Ömer, Osman and Ali and other distinguished personalities such as the Prophet's companions Ebul Hasan, Caferi Tayyar and Halid bin Velid. The sword of the Prophet has a hilt adorned with gold floral design and precious stones and a hilt guard in the form of a serpent. The scabbard of the sword is also decorated with precious stones. Another sword belonging to the Prophet bears the inscription "La ilahe illallah Muhammed Resulullah bin Abdullah bin Abdülmuttalip". The sword of Omer is plain and in the form of a snake, with the signature "Ibni Hattab." The sword of Osman has a double point and is sheathed in leather, with a gold hilt in the form of a lion's head. The sword of Ali is 112 centimeters long. These swords were later decorated with precious stones by the palace craftsmen. Behind the swords can be seen the locks and keys for the Tövbe Kapısı (Gate of Repentance) at the Kaaba.

On display in the showcase in the center of the room on the right is a piece of earth from the grave of the Prophet, the footprint 28 centimeters in length left by Muhammed when he ascended to heaven, which was brought from Tripoli in 1847 and placed in a gold frame; boxes containing hairs from Muhammed's beard; the agate seal of Muhammed 1 centimeter in length brought from Baghdad; a fragment of a tooth broken in the battle of Uhud; and the letter written in 627 by the Prophet to Mukavkıs, the

Seal of the prophet.

Holy Relics of the prophet.

Key of Kaaba.

ruler of the Egyptian Coptic community, inviting him to embrace Islam. This letter, consisting of 12 lines on brown parchment bearing the seal of Muhammed, was found in Egypt in 1850. Two of Muhammed's swords can be seen in front of the door leading from this room into the Chamber of the Holy Relics. On the ceiling there are candlesticks and pendants, the silver pendants being decorated with gold gilt and precious stones and ending in three large tassels. The mantle of the Prophet, 1.24 centimeter in length, with some parts missing, and made of black wool with wide sleeves, is preserved, in a gold chest inscribed with verses from the Koran set on a gold-plated table. The Prophet presented the mantle to the poet Kaab of Mecca on his acceptance of Islam, and although the Umayyad ruler Muaviye offered Kaab 10,000 silver pieces for the mantle, Kaab refused to sell. On Kaab's death, however, his children sold it to Muaviye for 20,000 silver pieces. The room also contains the Sancak-ı Şerif (the banner of the Prophet). When war was declared, the Sancak-ı Şerif was placed on the Sancak stone at the third gate in front of the Throne Room and a ceremony conducted consisting of the recitation of the Fatiha, the first sura of the Koran, followed by prayers, after which the banner was hand-ed over to the Grand Vizier. After the end of hostilities, the banner was brought back and returned to its former its place in the Chamber. Also to be seen here is the "Teyemmum Taşı," consisting of an Assyrian clay tablet with which Muhammed performed his ritual ablutions when no water could be found. Other holy relics include the staff of Muhhamed and his bow, preserved in a gold gilt box.

Holy relics.

The Library of Ahmet III

Though it is closed to visitors today, this library, which is located directly behind the Chamber of Petitions and in the center of the Third Court, attracts attention with its exterior appearance. This structure, which resembles a small mosque, was built at the beginning of the 18th century by Sultan Ahmet III, who took a great interest in reading. This library, which served the Enderun as a library until the time when the palace was no longer used, currently houses about 3,500 manuscripts, the most important of these are exhibited in the old Quarters of the Royal Guards, where the portraits of the Sultans are also found.

The structure sits on a high foundation in order to prevent the books from harmful humidity whereas because of its domed roof, it resembles a mosque when looked at from outside. The entrance, with its decorated with a wide and refreshing pavilion that rises over four columns, presents an appealing view as well as a sense of integrity with the stonework fountain positioned in front.

Baghdat pavilion and the pavilion "iftariye" of Sultan Ibrahim the "Mad".

The Fourth Court and the Pavilions

Baghdat pavilion.

Unlike the first three courts which are entered through splendid gates, the Palace's Fourth Court is entered through passages that are situated between the dormitory buildings of those connected to the enderun. This was because there were no security checks run at this point. As only the Sultan, his family and his closest officials were permitted past the Third Court, there wasn't the need for a separate control system. However, not all those connected with the Enderun could pass into the Fourth Court whenever they wished. Only those needed to submit services to the Sultan were permitted to enter. In addition, this fourth section, which was also known as "Hasbahçe" (Private Garden) was solely for the use of the Sultan.

Unlike the Second and Third Courts, the Fourth Court is not surrounded by colonnades. The site is uneven, consisting of a series of terraces adorned with pavilions, pools and gardens. From here a gate opens into the Fifth Court, which is now open to the general public as Gülhane Park.

On the left is the highest of the terraces, paved with white marble and with a pool with jet d'eau in one corner. In the vicinity of the pool are to be found the Circumcision Room and the Baghdad and Revan Pavilions. The area between the pool and the Chamber of the

Mantle of the Prophet is paved with colored mosaic. Built by Ibrahim the Mad in 1640, the Circumcision Room, or Sünnet Odası, consists of a single chamber with tile sheathing on both the interior and exterior. Some of the tiles date from the 17th century and are thus contemporary with the pavilion itself, while others, brought from other buildings, date from the 15th and 16th centuries. It was here

View of the Bagdat pavilion from the lower garden.

that the ceremony of the circumcision of the princes was performed, but the term "sünnet" refers to all religious practices derived from the Prophet's own practices and pronouncements and not only circumcision, and the name of this pavilion may have arisen from the custom of the sultans of performing the supererogatory part of the ritual prayer (Sünnet) in the "Sünnet Odası" (Circumcision Room) and the obligatory part (farz) in the Chamber of the Mantle of the Prophet. We also learn from documentary sources that the sultans were in the habit of conducting their daily business in this room.

Between the Circumcision Room and the Baghdad Pavilion stands the Iftariye erected by Ibrahim the Mad in 1641. This consists of a gazebo where the "iftar," the evening meal after the daily fast in Ramazan, was served and where the Sultan exchanged greetings with those closely related to him after the bayram prayers. The Baghdad Pavilion was erected by Sultan Murat IV in 1639. This pavilion, which is one of the most beautiful corners of the Topkapı Palace, was constructed to commemorate the conquest of Iraq and the Persian Gulf region. It is octagonal in shape with two doors and is surrounded by a portico with 22 columns. The exterior is sheathed in colored marble up to the level of the top of the windows and above that with tiles. There are two balconies, one looking out on to the Bosphorus and the other on to the Golden Horn. Miniature paintings show that these balconies were furnished with divans, cushions and carpets. The interior of the dome is one of the very rare extant examples of decoration on trowelled plaster work. The interior decoration of this place is of matchless beauty. The gold leaf dome decorations are the finest examples of their sort. The faience and tile craftsmanship is first class. The silver, mother-of-pearl and ivory inlay work which adorns the cabinet doors and other wooden material is extremely dazzling. A magnificent brazier which exhibits some very fine worksmanship along with the wrought copper fireplace situated between sofas are worth seeing. The hand woven carpets decorating the middle of the hall and sitting niches are amongst the finest examples of their kind.

The Revan Pavilion was built by Murat IV in 1635. As with the Bagdad Pavilion, this name of this pavilion, which is the Ottoman equivalent of Yerevan, commemorates the conquest of new territory in the Caucasian Mountains. Like the Baghdad Pavilion, it is built on an octagonal plan with marble and tile revetment on the exterior. It was here that the sultan's turbans were kept. On the 15th day of Ramazan, the holy relics would be brought here from the Chamber opposite, cleaned and returned to their former position. The Koran was recited in the Revan Pavilion during the process.

The Fil Bahçesi (Elephant Garden) and Incirlik Bahçesi (Fig Tree Garden) lie in the area towards the park 15 meters below the level of the terrace with the pool. Here we find the Sofa or Mustafa Pasha Pavilion, the Tower of the Head Physician, the Mecidiye Pavilion and the Robe Room. It was here that various varieties of tulip, the flower that gave its name to a whole period of Ottoman history, were cultivated and in which the most refined entertainments were held while the sultans looked on from their pavilions above. Some believe that the name of the garden was not Lâle (tulip) but Lala (royal tutor) and that the tower mentioned above was the tower, not of the Head Physician but of the Head Tutor. Probably both are acceptable. Sources show that it was only after the accession of Ahmet III that it became known as the Tulip Garden.

The date of construction of the Sofa Pavilion is uncertain but we know from documentary sources that the Russian Ambassador was received here in 1682, which means that the pavilion must have been constructed at an earlier date.

The Mecidiye Pavilion, the Robe Room and the Sofa Mosque on the right-hand side of the lowest terrace in the Fourth Court bring us to

Baghdat pavilion and the view of the "iftariye" of Sultan Ibrahim the "Mad" from the Revan kiosk.

the 19th century and the reign of Abdülmecit (1839-1861). The Mecidiye Pavilion was designed by Sarkis Balyan, the architect responsible for the design and construction of Dolmabahçe Palace and, as it was the last pavilion to be built in Topkapı Palace, it was also known as the New Pavilion (Yeni Köşk). The Çadır Köşkü (Tent Pavilion), which previously occupied the site, was demolished to make way for the new structure, but the foundations of the old pavilion were found to have been built over earlier Byzantine walls and the difference between the two methods of construction is very striking. We have no information regarding the function the pavilion was intended to perform. By the time of its construction the sultans no longer resided in the palace and rumor has it that Abdülmecit found the pavilion so little to his taste that he spent only a single night there.

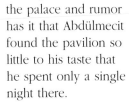

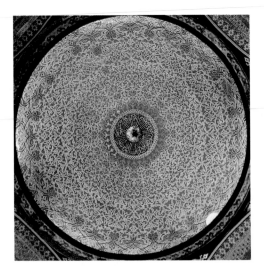

Above :
Outer courtyard gate of the Holy Relics.

Below :
Detail from a ceiling of the Palace.

The Final Word

As we have mentioned before, the Topkapı Palace will disappoint those guests who dream of finding a western style building with a definite, elaborate architecture and pompous decorations. But the guest will soon see, that it is one of the most prestigious and rich museums of the world with the collections exhibited in its halls.

The Topkapı Palace is also situated in an amazing spot that is unique in the world: It is at the tip of the last peninsula to the right of the point where the European continent ends. If you watch the sea from the courtyard near the Mecidiye Pavilion, the Asian side of İstanbul, that Anatolian İstanbul, is visible with all its splendour. A close watch from the same spot also reveals a 32-kilometer-long waterway, the Bosphorus, between Asia and Europe that is unsurpassed in beauty and history. The shores of the Bosphorus look as if the two continents extend their lips to each other with only a few hundreds of meters in between. The Bosphorus is also the Black Sea's only opening to the warm southern seas. The view from this spot is the full extention of southern Bosphorus up to the hanging Bosphorus Bridge with more than 1 kilometer between its feet.

On the other hand, the courtyard of the Baghdad Pavilion overlooks the Golden Horn and Galata. The view here shows the Golden Horn opening up to the Bosphorus and the never ending ebb and tide of traffic on both the land and in the sea. The Galata Tower built by Genoese merchants stands in the front. To the left of the tower, the Galata and Unkapanı bridges over the Golden Horn, the magnificent mosques of the Ottoman Age, the Beyazıt tower and the breath-taking panorama of one of the most beautiful metropoles in the world can charm any visitor...

The view of the palace from the sea is another sight too. The historic peninsula with the illuminated Topkapı Palace, the Ayasofya and the Blue Mosque near it glitters like the jewels of a crown especially on moonlit nights.

Let us repeat once more: Welcome to İstanbul.

REVAK

TOPKAPI PALACE

CONTENTS

Published and Distributed by

REHBER Basım Yayın Dağıtım Reklamcılık ve Tic. A.Ş.

Dolapdere Cad. No.106 Dolapdere-Şişli-Istanbul/TURKEY

Tel.: 0212 240 58 05   Fax: 0212 231 33 50

http:www.revak.com.tr

Text : Selçuk Tuzcuoğlu - T. Ahmet Şensılay

Photo : Rehber Basım Yayın Arşivi - Nadir Ede

Graphic and Layout : AS & 64 Ltd. Şti - Avni Alan

Colour Separation and Printed Turkey by : Asır Matbaacılık A.Ş.

ISBN 975-8212-39-7